DANA SETO

Making Money with AI

Start Your Side Hustle in 4 Steps

Copyright © 2025 by Dana Seto

All rights reserved. No part of this publication may be reproduced, stored or transmitted in any form or by any means, electronic, mechanical, photocopying, recording, scanning, or otherwise without written permission from the publisher. It is illegal to copy this book, post it to a website, or distribute it by any other means without permission.

First edition

This book was professionally typeset on Reedsy. Find out more at reedsy.com

Contents

1 Introduction	1
Why Now Is the Perfect Time to Start	2
What This Book Will Do for You	3
The Secret Weapon: AI Prompt Engineering	4
Before We Dive In	4
2 What is AI and How can I use it?	6
AI-Powered Economy and What It Means for You	6
The Best AI-Powered Side Hustle Ideas	9
3 Mastering AI Prompt Engineering Techniques	12
The Building Blocks of a Great Prompt	13
Experimenting with Variations and Context	15
Getting Started with AI Chatbots	18
4 Your First Experimental Project	20
Opportunity 1: Content Creation: Writing, Editing, and Storytelling	21
Opportunity 2: Visual Design: Graphics, Logos, and Presentation	23
Opportunity 3: Automation: Streaming Repetitive Business Tasks	26
5 Stay Ahead of the curve: Adapting in an Evolving Landscape	30
Embrace Lifelong Learning in AI	31
Stay Informed About AI Trends	34

	Integrate New AI Tools into Side Hustles	37
6	Bonus Material: 70+ "ACT AS" prompts that you can Copy and...	41
	Content Creator	41
	Visual Design	46
	Customer Communications	50
7	Conclusion: Your AI-Powered Side Hustle Awaits!	52
8	Appendix	54
9	Resources	55
10	Appendix 1 – 15 Ideas of Interest areas for AI-powered side...	58
11	Appendix 2 – Portfolio of Prompts	60

1

Introduction

If you have picked up this book, you probably have been thinking about ways to earn some extra income for a while. Well, I have some good news for you. This book will not only show ideas of what side hustles you can start, more specifically with AI (more on that later), but it will give you a structured system to guide you step-by-step to master AI prompts from zero knowledge or experience to a master user in 5 easy steps. Following these steps means you will achieve your 3 F's faster: flexibility, freedom and fun.

The AI-powered economy is exploding. OpenAI, the creator of ChatGPT reports that the generative AI brings in about $3 billion of revenue in 2024, up from zero a year ago. Investors are hungry and heavily investing in this sector. The global market for AI-powered economy is estimated to grow to $500 billion in the next few years. This opportunity is huge! This opportunity is not limited to tech start-ups. Look around you – from freelancers using AI to streamline tasks like writing and graphic design, to youtuber creating new content and courses, to entrepreneurs launching AI-driven eCommerce stores, the possibilities are endless. AI technology is changing how people make money and offering an opportunity for you to kickstart your side hustle ideas that you have been pounding (for a while).

This book is your guide to tapping into the incredible opportunity of the AI-powered economy, not in some far-off future, but right now. Whether you're in US, Canada, UK or anywhere else in the world, AI is creating possibilities that didn't exist just a few years ago. With a little creativity, the right tools, and a few key skills (that I'll teach you), you can be part of this new wave and start earning extra income in ways that fit your life.

Why Now Is the Perfect Time to Start

AI isn't just for tech geniuses or Silicon Valley insiders anymore. Tools like ChatGPT, MidJourney, and others have brought AI to the masses. These platforms are like having a virtual Swiss Army knife that can help you write, design, brainstorm, and problem-solve—all at the push of a button.

The best part? You don't need to be an AI expert or a programmer to use them. If you can type a sentence, you can use AI. In fact, millions of people are already doing it, using AI to create everything from freelance writing gigs to online shops, marketing agencies, and even digital art businesses. The playing field has been leveled, and the opportunity is enormous.

INTRODUCTION

What This Book Will Do for You

This book provides a structured, step-by-step guide that will take you from, "What's an AI prompt?" to confidently running your own AI-powered side hustle in just four steps. We'll break everything down so it's easy to follow and implement, with no prior experience required.

Here's what we'll cover:

Step 1: What is AI and How can I use it?
  Step 2: Mastering AI Prompts
  Step 3: Your First Experimental Project
  Step 4: Staying Ahead of the Curve

By the end of this book, you'll have mastered the art of AI prompt engineering. You'll know how to ask the right questions and give clear instructions to get the best results. This isn't just about side hustles—it's about equipping yourself with skills that can open doors for years to come. Here are 2 bonuses for you, at the back of this book, you will find:

- 70+ "Act as" prompts that you can copy and paste to kick off your learning with AI; and
- A template for you to build your own portfolio of prompts that you use for your side hustle

Also, you will find a number of pop up boxes throughout the book to bust the myth of AI along the way.

The Secret Weapon: AI Prompt Engineering

Here's the thing about AI: It's only as good as the prompts you give it. Think of prompts like instructions or recipes. If you know how to write a good one, you can unlock AI's full potential. Don't worry if that sounds intimidating; it's not. I'll show you exactly how to do it with plenty of examples and exercises along the way.

Imagine being able to:

- Draft professional-looking blog posts, marketing materials, or eBooks in minutes.
- Create custom designs or artwork for clients.
- Automate repetitive tasks so you can focus on the fun, creative parts of your hustle.
- Brainstorm new ideas or solve problems faster than ever before.

These are just a few of the things AI can help you do, and mastering prompts is the key to unlocking these possibilities.

Before We Dive In

If you've ever felt overwhelmed by technology or worried that you're "not techy enough," this book is for you. I've written it in plain language, with zero jargon and plenty of real-world examples. My goal is to make you feel like you're sitting down with a friend who's showing you the ropes—because that's exactly what we're doing here.

So, grab a notebook, a beverage of your choice and let's get

INTRODUCTION

started. Your four steps journey to launching an AI-powered side hustle begins now. Are you ready?

> **Key Take Away**
>
> With the help of AI tools, starting a side hustle is faster and easier than 5 years ago. This is your opportunity to turn your idea into money generating machine.

2

What is AI and How can I use it?

Artificial Intelligence (AI) is transforming how we work and live, offering tools that perform tasks requiring human intelligence, like understanding language, creating designs or even driving cars. At its core, AI is about building systems that learn from data and adapt their actions based on what they learn. You don't need to be a tech expert to use AI—modern tools make it accessible to everyone, including you.

AI-Powered Economy and What It Means for You

The AI-powered economy is creating opportunities like never before. For someone looking to start a side hustle, this means you can leverage cutting-edge tools to generate income without needing technical degree or large upfront investments.

A common myth is that AI will replace jobs, but in reality,

AI is more about collaboration than competition. Instead of taking over, AI boosts productivity and enhances quality by automating repetitive tasks and freeing up time for creativity and strategy. For example:

- **Content Creation**: Traditional methods of writing blog posts or marketing materials could take hours. With AI, you can draft high-quality content in minutes, allowing you to focus on tailoring it to your audience

- **Graphic Design**: Designing visuals used to require specialized skills and software. Today, tools like Canva or MidJourney enable anyone to create professional graphics quickly and easily.

- **Customer Service**: Chatbots powered by AI can handle routine inquiries 24/7, allowing businesses to focus on resolving complex customer needs.

By using AI, you can work smarter, not harder, turning what once were time-intensive tasks into opportunities to scale your efforts. This opens the door for anyone—no matter their background—to start a profitable side hustle with minimal barriers while delivering results that rival traditional methods.

> **MYTH: AI will replace many human jobs**
>
> REALITY: AI is designed to be used as a collaborative partner (or an assistant tool). Opposite of the believe that it will replace jobs. According to research, AI is estimated to create around 97 million emerging new roles in the AI sector as early as 2025. These jobs will focus on managing and improving AI systems rather than replacing human workers.

Getting Started with the Right Mindset

Success with AI starts with using it responsibly and approaching it as a tool to enhance your work, not as a full replacement for human creativity and insights. Here's how:

1. **Use AI as a Collaborative Partner**: AI is here to assist, not replace. Treat it as a tool that amplifies your skills and productivity. Relying solely on AI without adding your unique input risks creating generic, uninspired results.
2. **Refine Your Outputs**: AI-generated content or designs often need a human touch to ensure quality, accuracy, and personal relevance. Always review, edit, and refine AI outputs to align them with your vision and standards.
3. **Embrace Curiosity and Experimentation**: Treat this journey as an opportunity to explore. The more curious and willing you are to try new tools and techniques, the better equipped you'll be to unlock AI's full potential. Experimentation helps you discover what works best for your goals.
4. **Set a Clear Goal**: Define what you want to achieve with your AI-powered side hustle. Whether it's earning extra income, exploring a creative passion, or building a new skill, having a clear objective will guide your efforts and

keep you motivated.
5. **Be Willing to Learn**: Mistakes are part of the process. Each misstep is a learning opportunity that will bring you closer to mastering AI. Approach challenges with a growth mindset.
6. **Celebrate Progress**: Recognize and celebrate your wins, no matter how small. Each step forward—from testing a tool to completing your first project—is a milestone worth acknowledging.

Using AI responsibly ensures that your work stands out and maintains the authenticity and quality that only a human touch can bring. By combining your creativity with AI's capabilities, you create products and services that resonate with others and deliver real value.

Key Take Away

- You don't need any technical expertise to start an AI-powered side hustle. Many AI tools have intuitive, user-friendly interface that allow new users to start using the tools with no training. What you need to be successful in this endeavor is the willingness to start and continue to learn and adapt.

- Use AI as an assistant tool to help you speed up or enhance your work. Do not use it as a replacement to do your work. Always, Always, Always, review the output of AI outputs and put in your personal touch.

The Best AI-Powered Side Hustle Ideas

A step towards deciding what side hustle you can start by thinking about what you already know and what you are passionate about and think about how you want to share that information with others. For example, I am good at consulting, because that is my day job for over a decade AND I enjoy teaching. So, one of my side hustle ideas is to create an online course to teach consulting for others who aspire to become a consultant.

As you embrace on this journey, you need to remember that you don't need to be an expert in a field to start a side hustle, you just need to know more than someone else and you are passionate to share that knowledge with others.

Here are some ideas of AI-powered side hustles you can start:

- **Freelance Writing**: Use AI to draft and polish content.
- **Graphic Design**: Create stunning visuals for clients with AI tools.
- **Social Media Management**: Automate and streamline content creation.
- **Transcription Services**: Use AI transcription tools to quickly convert audio or video into text.
- **Online Tutoring or Coaching**: Use AI to create personalized lesson plans or automate administrative tasks for your tutoring business.
- **eBook Publishing**: Write and publish eBooks faster by leveraging AI for drafting and editing.
- **Virtual Assistance**: Offer administrative support enhanced by AI tools for scheduling, email drafting, and task management.
- **AI-Powered Market Research**: Use AI to analyze trends, gather insights, and provide actionable reports for clients.
- **Customized Gift Creation**: Use AI art tools to create unique, personalized gifts like digital portraits or themed graphics.

- **SEO Consulting**: Use AI to optimize websites for search engines by generating keywords, meta descriptions, and content ideas.

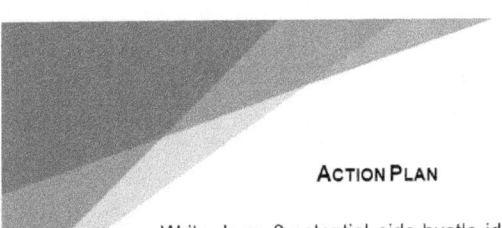

ACTION PLAN

Write down 3 potential side hustle ideas that you think you can do

p.s. If you are feeling stuck, refer to Appendix 1 at the back of the book for some ideas and see which one jumps out at you

What are the 3 side hustle ideas that jump out at you?

1. _____

2. _____

3. _____

3

Mastering AI Prompt Engineering Techniques

The best way to go through this chapter is to follow along, copying the prompts provided in this book and pasting them into an AI chatbot to see the output. There are many free AI chatbots available that you can choose from, with ChatGPT being the most popular. If you want other options, you can simply google "ChatGPT alternatives free" and you will get a list of all available options. Once you picked a tool, sign up for a free account, and you are ready to start experimenting and learning this fundamental, yet future-proof skills in the world of AI.

AI prompt engineering is the art of crafting effective instructions to get the most out of AI tools. For some readers who already have some experience AI chatbots, you might wonder why sometimes the chatbot will give you generic answers while other times you are getting a very thorough and easy to understand response. The magic lies in what I called the "building blocks of a great prompt. This chapter will show you what an AI prompt is and how to craft a great prompt. We can walk through a few examples together. By the end of this chapter, you will have mastered the skills of crafting a killer AI prompt and start building your portfolio of prompts that you can use in your side hustle.

The Building Blocks of a Great Prompt

A great prompt has six components, not all components are mandatory, but the more concise your components are, the higher the quality of the output you will get from the AI chatbot. The six components are:

- Persona
- Context
- Task
- Exemplars
- Format
- Tone

Generally speaking, the first three components (Persona, Context, and Task) are mandatory to create a great prompt, where as the remaining three components (Exemplars, Format, Tone) are considered as optional.

Let's use the following example to see what it means:
"Act as a senior marketing manager at a giant tech company

and you just launched the latest innovation product, an augmented reality goggles for remote collaborations, and received 10,000 pre-orders, which is 20% higher than target.

Write an email to your boss, sharing this positive news. The email should follow the same format as I will share in the attachment. Use clear and concise language and write in a confident yet friendly tone.

<attached a sample format>"

Using the sample prompt above, you can see:

- Persona – Act as a senior marketing manager at a giant tech company
- Context – launched the latest innovation product, an augmented reality goggles for remote collaborations, and received 10,000 pre-orders, which is 20% higher than target
- Task – write an email to your boss, sharing the positive news
- Exemplars – <attached a sample format>
- Format – the email should follow the same format as I will share in the attachment
- Tone – use clear and concise language and write in a confident yet friendly tone

If you are following along, you may choose to skip out on the "attached a sample format>" step, but the message here is, this is an example of a great prompt that will generate a high-quality output. It consists of the structure by offering all 6 components of what a great prompt need, the prompt was written with clear, logical and detailed instructions; therefore it provided a set of very clear instructions for the AI tools to follow and generate a response.

Experimenting with Variations and Context

A great prompt often requires multiple iterations of the six components we spoke about to allow AI chatbot to generate an informative response. One key message to keep in mind when using AI tools is <u>Never Copy and Paste</u> exactly what AI gives you and call it your own work. You should always review the work generated by AI and put in your own touch to create the final product.

Let's go through a couple examples of how we can iterate our prompts into a killer prompt.

Example 1:

Let's say you are researching for a presentation for your client and want to understand what the key benefits are of using renewable energy.

Original prompt: "Can you list benefits of renewable energy?"

What do you think of this prompt? Does it have all the six components that we spoke about? If not, how might you want to improve it? Try adding a persona to the prompt as first step.

Iteration #1: "As a consultant, I want to understand the benefits of renewable energy. Can you create a list of benefits of renewable energy."

Ok, what responses did the AI chatbot gives you? Are you satisfied with that answer? This iteration now contains a persona and a task, but is there any refinement you want to make further? How about adding some more context to the prompt?

Iteration #2: "As a consultant, reflecting on the 2022 climate conference, I would like to present the benefits of renewal energy to my client to encourage them to move towards renewable energy in their new project. Can you review the attached conference material and create a bulletin list of benefits of using renewal energy in urban planning?"

How is the response now? As you can see every iteration will reveal additional insights. This is because AI chatbot is generally using the information you input and continue to build (or "train") their response back to you.

Example #2:

In this example, you would like the AI chatbot to summarize a 100 page medical doctor that you received from your doctor and trying to understand what it means.

One of the first thing to note is depending on the AI chatbot you use, there is different policy on how data you input are treated in training the AI model. Some models will use your input documents and trains its model, meaning the information you put in could become public information. While some models are not using your input to train the model. Ensure you check out each company's website before deciding if you want to share your information with the tool at hand.

Original prompt: "Summarize this report for me"

While there is nothing wrong with the task oriented prompt in this example. The tool could probably give you a summary in paragraph format. One thing you can try to iterate this prompt on is the persona, tone to make the response more useful.

Iteration #1: "As a daily care giver, I want to understand my patient's health condition so I can provide the best support to them. Can you please summarize this report for me?"

Noticed how adding a person and changing the tone to be more polite changes the output of the AI generated response? What if now you want to be able to copy this summary in a log book for future reference. Let's iterate on it again.

Iteration #2: "As a daily care giver, I want to understand my patient's health condition so I can provide the best support them. Can you please summarize this report for me? The format of the response should be in bullet point, outlining a focus area for each bullet point."

There, you have it!

The key to generating a killer prompt is to the iteration of refinement. As you see in the examples above, the more you refine the prompt, the more clear and more targeted the output you will receive from AI.

Now, I encourage you to take some of your real life examples, and practice creating prompts and iterate on them.

> **Key Take Away**
>
> - An effective AI prompt consists of six components: Persona, Context, Task, Exemplars, Format and Tone. While not all components are required to generate a response, usually the more relevant infomation you provided to AI, the less generic the output will be.
>
> - To generate an informative response from AI, users often need to go through multiple iterations of prompt engineering. These additional tweaks you make to the prompt will help reveal additional insights as you interact with the AI tool.

Getting Started with AI Chatbots

Getting started with AI chatbots involves some initial setup procedures. While the technical aspect may seem daunting, many platforms offer user-friendly interfaces that guide you through the process. Typically, the first step is selecting a chatbot provider that aligns with your needs. The options vary widely, from simple rule-based bots to sophisticated AI-driven solutions. Once you've chosen a provider, you'll configure the chatbot according to your specific requirements, which often includes defining the conversation flow and integrating the bot with existing systems like CRM or help desks.

For non-technical professionals eager to dive into this technology, signing up for a free AI chatbot service can provide invaluable hands-on experience. These services often come with intuitive dashboards that allow beginners to experiment with creating simple chatbots without coding expertise. By starting small and gradually scaling up, users can learn the ropes at their own pace while observing how automated conversations unfold in real-time.

Here are some beginner friendly and free AI chatbot you might want to sign up and start experimenting with prompt engineering:

- ChatGPT 4.o
- Google Gemini
- Microsoft Copilot
- Claude
- Perplexity AI

ACTION PLAN

- Choose an AI chatbot and sign up for a free account
- Write 3 prompts and iterate through prompt engineering
- Start building your own prompt portfolio (see Appendix 2 for a bonus template)

4

Your First Experimental Project

Exploring AI-powered side hustles is a thrilling venture that opens up numerous opportunities across various fields. Embracing AI in your side hustle can redefine how you approach and execute your ideas, offering innovative solutions and efficiency boosts that traditional methods might lack. The intersection of AI and entrepreneurship allows even non-technical professionals to dive into new ventures with tools that simplify complex tasks. This chapter invites you to explore the myriad of ways AI can transform your side hustle dreams into reality, showing how AI has become an essential ally in this modern age of innovation.

As you delve deeper into this chapter, you'll discover how AI technologies are being leveraged in several industries, creating unique side hustle openings that weren't possible before. We'll journey through content creation, where AI aids in writing and editing, making it accessible to everyone, not just professional writers. Visual design also benefits from AI advancements, enabling even beginners to craft stunning graphics without the usual steep learning curve. Additionally, we'll touch on how AI can streamline repetitive business tasks, freeing up your time for more strategic endeavors. Each section will provide insights into these captivating areas, equipping you with the knowledge to identify and pursue AI-driven opportunities that align with your interests and career goals.

Opportunity 1: Content Creation: Writing, Editing, and Storytelling

In today's digital age, artificial intelligence (AI) is rapidly becoming a significant player in content creation, offering unique and valuable opportunities as a side hustle. Whether you're looking to break into freelance writing or you run a small business, AI tools can be your new best friend, especially when creating compelling written content. These tools don't just streamline the process; they revolutionize it, making writing accessible even to those who might not consider themselves natural-born writers.

One of the primary benefits of AI in writing is its ability to expedite drafting and editing processes. This is crucial for anyone juggling a main job and a side gig. Tools like Grammarly and Jasper.ai, powered by AI, help individuals draft articles or blog posts quickly and efficiently. With automated suggestions for improving grammar, style, and clarity, these tools significantly cut down the time spent on producing initial drafts. This positions AI as an ally for those seeking to make the most of their limited schedule, allowing them to focus more energy on creative aspects and less on technical corrections.

Moreover, Natural Language Processing (NLP) takes AI's role in content creation up a notch by enhancing storytelling capabilities. NLP, a fascinating branch of AI, provides creative prompts and generates unique narratives, sparking inspiration for writers everywhere. For example, if you're developing a storyline for a blog post or short story, AI can suggest plot developments or even dialogue options that align with your intended theme. This capability not only aids in overcoming writer's block but also opens avenues for crafting innovative, engaging stories that capture readers' attention. Whether you're a seasoned writer or just starting, the creative boost from NLP ensures your voice remains fresh and captivating.

Adding another layer of sophistication, AI employs machine learning algorithms to tailor content to specific audiences. This personalization significantly enhances engagement rates, an essential factor for bloggers, marketers, and anyone relying on digital media to reach their audience. For instance, AI tools can analyze data such as past user interactions or trending topics within a particular niche, offering insights into what content will likely resonate with readers. By understanding preferences, AI allows creators to deliver tailored messages that speak directly to individual interests or needs, fostering a stronger connection between the creator and the audience. Such tailored communication is invaluable, particularly in an era where personal branding and curated messaging are key to standing out amid the noise of online content.

The integration of AI into content creation heralds a new era of possibilities for those interested in pursuing this avenue as a side hustle. It democratizes access to quality writing resources, reducing the gap between amateur writers and professional-grade output. No longer confined to traditional methods, individuals can now harness the power of AI to generate polished, compelling content in less time, freeing up moments to diversify their efforts or pursue additional creative endeavors.

Furthermore, AI's versatility means it's applicable across various content types. Beyond mere text generation, AI tools optimize product descriptions, social media posts, emails, and even chatbot responses, making them ideal for a range of scenarios. This diversity offers multiple revenue streams within the content creation sphere, catering to different interests and specialties. As AI evolves, its applications will expand further, opening doors to novel ways of engaging with audiences, while maintaining efficiency and efficacy.

Opportunity 2: Visual Design: Graphics, Logos, and Presentation

To harness the potential of AI in visual design projects effectively, it's essential first to ask, "What problem will you solve with AI?" Acknowledging this question as a guiding principle can direct our focus towards meaningful challenges that AI can address in the realm of design. One immediate advantage that

AI brings to the table is its capacity to simplify graphics creation tasks, making it extremely beneficial for those looking to dive into side hustles centered around graphic design.

AI-driven tools like Canva are excellent examples of how technology can streamline and democratize design tasks. These platforms offer pre-designed templates that make creating visually appealing content—such as logos and social media posts—a straightforward process. Even without a formal design background, users can achieve professional-grade results by leveraging these templates. The intuitive nature of these tools reduces the steep learning curve traditionally associated with graphic design software, thereby opening doors for non-designers to participate in creative projects efficiently. Embracing such tools not only saves time but also empowers individuals to take on more projects, ultimately translating into additional income streams for many aspiring designers.

As we delve deeper into artificial intelligence in design, Generative Adversarial Networks (GANs) emerge as revolutionary contributors. GANs operate by pitting two neural networks against each other to generate new, creative content. For designers, this means an innovative partner capable of producing unique visuals by experimenting with various styles and patterns. The creative opportunities provided by GANs can elevate one's portfolio, offering fresh perspectives and designs that stand out in competitive markets. Designers can utilize GANs to discover aesthetics they may never have attempted manually, thus extending their artistic capabilities while remaining efficient. This aspect of AI allows designers to work smarter, not harder, when developing their visual projects.

Moreover, AI does wonders in presentation design. This seemingly mundane task often requires hours of structuring and fine-tuning to convey messages effectively. AI tools now possess the capability to enhance this process significantly. By analyzing the content input, these tools can intelligently suggest suitable layout options and incorporate relevant visual elements seamlessly. This not only guarantees a cohesive aesthetic throughout the presentation but also ensures that key points are highlighted in visually compelling ways. Users can produce polished presentations with minimal effort, making it easier to handle multiple clients or projects simultaneously. Here again, AI steps in as a formidable ally, freeing up time for other creative endeavors while ensuring consistent quality across outputs.

As exciting as these advancements are, integrating AI into design requires transparency and careful consideration of client needs. Some clients might have policies against using AI-generated content, fearing detachment from their brand personality. Thus, it becomes crucial to communicate openly about the extent to which AI influences your work. Ensuring that the output aligns with a client's brand narrative may require additional human touch and refinement. This delicate balance between AI efficiency and personalized service is where the true skill lies, distinguishing successful designers in the AI era.

When setting up your AI resources, it's important to recognize the technological landscape and identify suitable tools that complement your specific objectives. Whether it's through mastering a particular AI design tool or exploring varied functionalities across platforms, having a strategic setup ensures that you're ready to tackle diverse design challenges. The ability to pivot and adapt based on project requirements can be enhanced through familiarization with a range of AI capabilities, allowing you to choose the right tool for the right task. In this way, AI doesn't just automate processes; it equips designers with a versatile toolkit tailored for innovation and creativity.

In essence, exploring AI-powered visual design opens an array of income-generating possibilities for those willing to engage with evolving technologies. From crafting striking visuals effortlessly with tools like Canva to employing sophisticated methods via GANs, the prospective avenues are numerous. As the AI landscape continues to evolve, designers who stay informed and curious about new developments will find themselves at the forefront of this dynamic field.

Opportunity 3: Automation: Streaming Repetitive Business Tasks

In today's fast-paced world, finding ways to efficiently manage time and tasks can lead to profitable side hustles—especially when leveraging the power of artificial intelligence (AI). One such area where AI shines is in automating mundane tasks that often bog down individuals and businesses. By utilizing AI technologies like Robotic Process Automation (RPA), chatbots, and scheduling tools, we can turn routine chores into opportunities for income.

Robotic Process Automation (RPA) is a game-changer when it comes to handling repetitive tasks. Think about data entry—a task that's not only tedious but also prone to human errors. With RPA, these processes can be completed accurately and swiftly without the usual hiccups. It operates by using software robots to mimic human interactions with digital systems and applications, thus speeding up processes that would otherwise demand significant manual effort. This technology saves time and minimizes errors, making it a perfect tool for anyone looking to automate tasks as part of their side hustle. Many companies are already implementing RPA to optimize operations, which means there's a growing market for freelance RPA services.

Another exciting development is the use of AI chatbots in customer service. These bots provide support at any hour, addressing common questions without needing a human agent. They can handle inquiries, process orders, and even troubleshoot issues, leaving more complex problems for humans to resolve. For those interested in building an AI-powered side hustle, setting up chatbot services for businesses offers an excellent opportunity. As companies strive to enhance customer experiences and cut operational costs, learning to deploy and maintain chatbots can be both lucrative and fulfilling.

Then there's the integration of AI into scheduling and email management. We all know how managing emails and appointments can feel like a full-time job. With AI tools, you can automate these tasks, ensuring that emails are sorted, prioritized, and responded to with minimal delay. Scheduling tools powered by AI can help in optimizing meeting times, taking into account participants' availability and preferences. By employing these tools, businesses not only save time but also allow professionals to dedicate more time to strategic and creative endeavors. Offering consulting services on how to integrate these AI solutions could become a profitable venture.

To get started, it's important to first identify which tasks in your personal or professional life could benefit from automation. Consider trying out different AI platforms to see which aligns best with your needs. Documenting each problem you're aiming to solve with AI and keeping this information handy is crucial. Not only does it ensure you stay focused, but it also helps in tracking progress and outcomes, providing valuable insights into what works best as you refine your strategies.

Key Take Away

- The most common AI-powered side hustle includes
    - Content Creation
    - Visual Design
    - Tasks Automation

- To decide which AI-powered side hustle you should start, consider the question:
    "What problem do you enjoy solving?"

ACTION PLAN

Complete the questions below and revisiting the 3 ideas of side hustles you wrote down from Chapter 1, pick one side hustle that you want to start after finish reading this book.

1. What problem do you enjoy solving while getting paid:

   _____

2. Out of my original 3 ideas of side hustle, I want to start this one:

   _____

3. My motivation for starting this side hustle is:

   _____

4. The AI-tools I need to start this side hustle include:

   _____

5. What practice project(s) can I do to dip my toes into this side hustle?
   (For example: if you want to be a blogger, try using AI tools to research blog ideas, and draft your first blog)

   _____

6. I commit to complete this practice project by (date):

   _____

5

Stay Ahead of the curve: Adapting in an Evolving Landscape

Congratulations on completing your first practice project! With the completed action plan from last chapter, I am confident that you now have a clear roadmap to start your AI-powered side hustle. But before you do that, I want to provide some information that can help you stay ahead of the rapidly evolving field of AI.

Staying ahead in the AI game isn't just about keeping up with what's new—it's about actively seeking out ways to adapt and incorporate advancements into your work. The landscape of artificial intelligence is rapidly changing, and for those who are looking to dive into AI-powered ventures, this brings both opportunities and challenges. You might find yourself wondering how best to navigate this evolving world and make the most of what AI has to offer. That's precisely where having a solid strategy comes into play, ensuring that you're not just a spectator but an active participant in harnessing AI's potential.

This chapter offers a treasure trove of insights and strategies designed to help you keep pace with AI developments while establishing your side hustle. We'll walk through various approaches, from embracing lifelong learning habits that keep your skills sharp, to integrating the latest AI tools into your business efficiently. You'll discover how to stay informed about emerging trends without getting overwhelmed, and how connecting with AI communities can be a game-changer in your journey. With this guide, you'll be well-equipped to explore new ventures with confidence, armed with the knowledge and tools you need to succeed in this dynamic field.

Embrace Lifelong Learning in AI

Developing a proactive learning mindset is key to staying ahead in the fast-paced world of artificial intelligence. Imagine you're about to start a new AI-powered side hustle; it's crucial to keep your skills fresh and relevant. One effective way to do this is by identifying online courses, webinars, and workshops specifically focused on AI. The internet is teeming with resources that cater to various levels of expertise, from beginner to advanced. Platforms like Coursera, edX, and Udacity offer structured courses, while sites like Eventbrite list AI-focused webinars and workshops. These resources not only help you understand current trends but also equip you with the tools needed for practical application.

Take some time to explore these options and see which ones align with your goals and interests. Are you interested in understanding machine learning algorithms, or are you more excited about data visualization techniques? Whatever your interest, there's likely a course out there for you! And remember, many courses provide certificates upon completion, adding a nice badge of accomplishment to your professional profile. This can be particularly beneficial when you're looking to impress potential clients or partners in your new venture.

Another vital component of developing a proactive learning mindset is engaging with AI communities and forums. In these spaces, you'll find a treasure trove of insights, shared experiences, and even challenges faced by others venturing into AI. Online communities such as Reddit's r/MachineLearning or specialized forums like those at Towards Data Science serve as excellent places to ask questions, share your projects, and learn from the successes and failures of others. These interactions can expand your understanding and spark new ideas for your own projects.

You might wonder how this exchange of knowledge is beneficial. Well, think of it as collective problem-solving. Within these communities, members often discuss real-world applications of AI, providing perspectives that books and courses alone cannot. Engaging regularly allows you to stay updated with the latest developments and emerging trends directly from those immersed in the field. Furthermore, being part of a community helps in building your professional network, an asset that could be invaluable when launching your side business.

Now, amidst all this learning and networking, it's essential to carve out time for self-study and skill updates in machine learning and data analytics. Setting aside regular, dedicated time for studying ensures consistent progress and prevents knowledge from becoming stagnant. Maybe you allocate an hour every morning before work, or perhaps Sunday afternoons become your study session times. Consistency is key here!

When contemplating what to study, focus on areas that will have direct impacts on your venture. Perhaps deepening your understanding of natural language processing would enhance your project, or maybe delving into predictive analytics could give you an edge over competitors. Prioritize learning that aligns with your immediate goals but don't shy away from exploring topics that might pique your curiosity — sometimes the most unexpected skills prove to be the most valuable.

Balancing coursework, community engagement, and self-study may seem daunting at first, but creating a realistic and flexible learning schedule can make it manageable. Consider setting small, achievable milestones to track your progress and maintain motivation. Perhaps your first goal is to complete an introductory course, followed by implementing a small AI model based on what you've learned.

While tackling these strategies, remember the significance of identifying reliable sources for AI updates. It's critical to ensure the information you consume and the skills you acquire are grounded in truth and relevance. Look for endorsements from experts in the field or affiliations with reputable institutions when choosing resources. Being discerning about your sources increases the value of your learning efforts, allowing you to stay on top of credible advancements in AI.

Adopting a proactive learning mindset isn't a one-time task—it's an ongoing process. As AI continues to evolve, so must your approach to learning. Embrace the journey, welcome change, and relish in the continual discovery AI presents. Whether you're a newcomer or a seasoned professional, cultivating a commitment to lifelong learning will undoubtedly set you apart in the bustling world of AI-driven innovation.

Stay Informed About AI Trends

In today's rapidly evolving technological landscape, staying current with AI developments is more crucial than ever, particularly for non-technical professionals eager to venture into AI-powered side businesses. One of the most effective ways to remain informed is by subscribing to reputable tech news sources and journals dedicated to AI. These publications offer in-depth coverage of the latest advancements, providing insights that are both accessible and comprehensive. For instance, outlets like Wired, TechCrunch, and MIT Technology Review regularly feature articles about new AI tools, ethical considerations, and breakthrough discoveries. Subscribing to these can ensure you receive a steady stream of curated content delivered straight to your inbox.

When exploring which sources to follow, consider those with a proven track record of accuracy and thought leadership. Choosing well-regarded publications means you're not just getting news; you're receiving expert analysis that delves into what these developments mean for industries across the board. Such insights are invaluable for identifying emerging trends that might impact your business ideas or provide avenues for innovation.

Beyond traditional publications, diving into the world of social media can be incredibly beneficial for real-time updates. Following influential AI experts and thought leaders on platforms such as Twitter and LinkedIn grant you access to a wide array of perspectives and discussions happening live. Thought leaders often share unique insights and analyses, enriching your understanding of how various AI technologies can be applied practically.

Engaging with their posts can also expose you to a broader community of followers who are similarly engaged in the AI sector. This interaction can foster rich dialogues, opening up opportunities to ask questions, gain clarity on complex issues, or even collaborate on projects. It's important to identify individuals whose viewpoints resonate with or challenge your understanding of AI. By curating a list of well-informed voices, you can deepen your engagement with current trends and debates shaping the field.

In addition to digital subscriptions and social media engagement, attending industry conferences and events remains one of the most impactful ways to stay ahead of AI advancements. These gatherings, whether in-person or virtual, offer a platform to hear directly from pioneers and innovators driving change in AI. Conferences such as NeurIPS, TEDxAI, or local tech meetups provide a wealth of knowledge through keynote speeches, panel discussions, and workshops tailored towards various levels of expertise.

Participating in these events can be immensely rewarding as they often highlight cutting-edge research, feature product demonstrations, and showcase successful case studies. Moreover, these are opportunities to network with industry peers, fostering partnerships or simply exchanging ideas that can be instrumental in developing your AI-enabled ventures. The chance to discuss shared interests with fellow attendees expands your professional circle and enhances your understanding of how different sectors are leveraging AI.

While these strategies provide foundational methods for staying informed, it's important not to overlook the value of participating in online AI communities. Engaging with forums and discussion groups allows for an exchange of ideas and solutions among practitioners worldwide. Platforms such as Reddit's machine learning community or Facebook's AI-focused groups serve as hubs for ongoing conversation, where members share resources, pose questions, and solve problems collaboratively.

To make the most out of these interactions, actively contribute by sharing your experiences or asking questions relevant to your field. This active participation cultivates a sense of belonging within the community and helps build a network of contacts who could become valuable collaborators or mentors as you navigate your AI journey.

Similarly, attending workshops and webinars provides structured learning opportunities designed to enhance your understanding of AI applications. Webinars hosted by renowned universities or industry experts allow you to delve into specific topics without the need for travel. These sessions often provide practical insights into deploying AI solutions, making them particularly useful for those considering how to incorporate AI into their side businesses.

Integrate New AI Tools into Side Hustles

In today's fast-paced world, starting an AI-powered side hustle can be both exciting and daunting. The key is figuring out how to leverage these technologies effectively in your entrepreneurial ventures. First, consider the various roles AI tools might play in your business. For instance, you could use AI for automating mundane tasks that take up your time or implementing an intelligent customer interaction system like chatbots. These applications aren't just about boosting efficiency; they're about freeing you up to focus on what truly matters – growing your business.

Before diving headfirst into new AI technology, it's crucial to assess its suitability for your specific needs. Not every AI solution will fit seamlessly into your business model. Take a deep dive into understanding what each tool offers and how it aligns with your goals. If you're running an e-commerce business, AI-driven analytics might help by providing insights into consumer behavior, whereas AI chatbots can enhance customer service. Always match the tool to the task at hand, ensuring it complements and enhances your existing processes.

Once you've identified potential AI tools, the next step is experimentation through pilot projects. These are small-scale tests that allow you to gauge the effectiveness of the AI solutions within your actual business environment without committing significant resources upfront. Pilot projects can reveal invaluable insights about how AI integrates into your workflow and can highlight potential challenges before they become major issues. This hands-on approach also provides a chance to gather feedback from team members and customers, helping refine the integration process.

A structured guideline can aid in effectively integrating AI tools into your workflow. Start by defining clear objectives for what you want to achieve with the AI implementation. Establish milestones and set realistic timelines for the pilot phase. Additionally, identify metrics that signify success, such as improved response times or increased customer satisfaction, and monitor these closely throughout the trial.

Experimenting with AI doesn't stop at pilot projects; it involves a mindset of ongoing exploration. The tech landscape evolves continuously, and staying open to new AI applications can keep your business ahead of the curve. Encourage an environment where testing and tinkering are part of the culture. Whether it involves trying out emerging AI software or exploring different algorithms, maintaining flexibility will enable you to adapt quickly to new advancements.

While experimenting, it's essential not to overlook the importance of evaluating performance and outcomes. Consistent evaluation helps in understanding what's working and what isn't. Examine the data collected during pilot projects and beyond, focusing on areas like cost reductions, time savings, and customer feedback. Based on this evaluation, you can make informed decisions about scaling up successful initiatives or tweaking those that need improvement.

Set up a mechanism for regular reviews of performance metrics like ROI, customer engagement rates, and operational efficiencies post-integration. This continuous assessment allows you to fine-tune your strategies and ensure the AI tools deliver the desired benefits. Remember, optimization is an ongoing process, requiring attention and a willingness to pivot when necessary.

One practical example is leveraging AI in customer service. Implementing AI chatbots can streamline communication by handling routine inquiries while allowing human agents to focus on complex issues. Pilot testing with a segment of your customer base can help fine-tune the chatbot's responses and gauge customer satisfaction levels. Analyzing these interactions provides valuable insights, enabling you to improve the AI system continuously.

Continuously refining AI integrations also involves staying updated with technological advancements. By keeping an eye on industry trends and innovating accordingly, you can ensure that your AI-powered venture remains relevant and competitive. Engage with tech communities or attend online workshops to stay abreast of the latest developments and best practices.

Incorporating AI into your business shouldn't be seen as a one-time project but rather an evolving journey. It's about learning, adapting, and growing alongside technology. Begin by understanding the potential applications and proceed with caution through pilot projects, mindful of matching technologies with business needs. Regular evaluations and adaptations should reflect a commitment to leveraging AI's full potential, focusing on creating value and enhancing operations.

Key Take Away

- AI is rapidly evolving – think of your AI-powered side hustle as a continuous improvement project. Dedicate time to stay on top of the trends and applications of emerging new AI-tools.

6

Bonus Material: 70+ "ACT AS" prompts that you can Copy and Paste

As a bonus, this chapter provides a list of 50+ prompts that are ready-made to help you quickly get started with AI chatbots. Remember you can always iterate to get a more clear output based on your context. Hope this will give you a head start.

Content Creator

Social Media Strategist

1. *"Act as a social media strategist. Create a 30-day content plan for a fitness influencer on Instagram, focusing on engagement and growth."*
2. *"Act as a social media strategist. Suggest ideas for a TikTok*

campaign to promote a sustainable fashion brand, targeting Gen Z."
3. *"Act as a social media strategist. Develop a strategy for increasing Twitter engagement for a tech blog, including types of tweets and posting schedules."*

SEO Expert

1. *"Act as an SEO expert. Identify long-tail keywords and content ideas for a blog about remote work, targeting working professionals."*
2. *"Act as an SEO expert. Suggest strategies to optimize existing content for a health and wellness website to improve search rankings."*
3. *"Act as an SEO expert. Create a list of 10 blog topics that could rank well for a photography business targeting wedding clients."*

Video Scriptwriter

1. *"Act as a video scriptwriter. Write a 60-second script for a social media ad promoting a meal delivery service, emphasizing convenience and quality."*
2. *"Act as a video scriptwriter. Develop a script for a 5-minute YouTube tutorial on how to use Canva for beginners."*
3. *"Act as a video scriptwriter. Create a storyboard for an animated explainer video about the benefits of a productivity*

app."

Email Marketing Specialist

1. *"Act as an email marketing specialist. Write a welcome email sequence for new subscribers to a newsletter about personal finance."*
2. *"Act as an email marketing specialist. Create a Black Friday email campaign for an online bookstore, highlighting discounts and exclusive offers."*
3. *"Act as an email marketing specialist. Draft a re-engagement email to inactive customers of a subscription box service, offering a special incentive to return."*

Visual Content Creator

1. *"Act as a visual content creator. Provide concepts for three Instagram carousel posts explaining the benefits of meditation."*
2. *"Act as a visual content creator. Design an infographic layout for '5 Tips for Effective Time Management' aimed at college students."*
3. *"Act as a visual content creator. Suggest ideas for Pinterest pins that promote a blog about DIY home decor projects."*

Brand Storyteller

1. *"Act as a brand storyteller. Write a compelling brand story for a startup that makes biodegradable packaging for everyday use."*
2. *"Act as a brand storyteller. Develop a narrative for an ad campaign highlighting the journey of an artist using a new drawing tablet."*
3. *"Act as a brand storyteller. Create a story-based social media post for a small business celebrating its 10th anniversary."*

Podcast Host

1. *"Act as a podcast host. Plan an episode discussing 'The Pros and Cons of Freelancing in 2024,' including key talking points and guest suggestions."*
2. *"Act as a podcast host. Create an engaging script for the introduction of a podcast episode on 'AI Tools Every Creator Should Know About.'"*
3. *"Act as a podcast host. Suggest a format and content flow for an interview with a best-selling author about their writing process."*

Meme Creator

1. *"Act as a meme creator. Generate three meme ideas that humorously highlight the challenges of starting a side hustle."*
2. *"Act as a meme creator. Create relatable meme concepts about*

the life of content creators for Instagram or Twitter."

3. *"Act as a meme creator. Develop a viral meme idea for a coffee brand targeting millennials, playing on 'morning struggles.'"*

Content Repurposing Expert

1. *"Act as a content repurposing expert. Suggest ways to turn a popular blog post about 'Healthy Meal Prep' into a series of TikTok videos and Instagram Reels."*
2. *"Act as a content repurposing expert. Provide a plan to convert a 20-minute podcast episode about productivity hacks into a YouTube video, a blog post, and social media content."*
3. *"Act as a content repurposing expert. Outline steps to repurpose a webinar on digital marketing into a lead magnet, blog series, and email campaign."*

Digital Marketing Analyst

1. *"Act as a digital marketing analyst. Analyze the performance of a Facebook ad campaign for a small business and suggest ways to improve ROI."*
2. *"Act as a digital marketing analyst. Provide insights on how to optimize Google Ads for an e-commerce store selling sustainable home products."*
3. *"Act as a digital marketing analyst. Recommend tools and strategies for tracking the performance of an influencer marketing campaign on Instagram."*

Visual Design

Logo Designer

1. *"Act as a logo designer. Suggest a modern and professional logo concept for a cybersecurity company called 'SecureSphere' that emphasizes trust and innovation."*
2. *"Act as a logo designer. Design a whimsical and hand-drawn logo idea for an organic bakery called 'Flour Power,' targeting a family-friendly audience."*
3. *"Act as a logo designer. Develop a geometric and dynamic logo for a sports brand named 'Pulse Gear,' focusing on energy and movement."*

Web Designer

1. *"Act as a web designer. Create a homepage layout for a non-profit organization focused on clean water initiatives, highlighting donation options and impact stories."*
2. *"Act as a web designer. Suggest a design structure for a travel agency's website that emphasizes destination packages and customer testimonials."*
3. *"Act as a web designer. Outline a responsive design concept for a blog dedicated to interior design trends, ensuring mobile and desktop compatibility."*

UI/UX Designer

1. *"Act as a UI/UX designer. Design a user interface for an e-learning platform, focusing on intuitive navigation and engaging course previews."*
2. *"Act as a UI/UX designer. Suggest a wireframe for a budgeting app that offers real-time expense tracking and saving goals."*
3. *"Act as a UI/UX designer. Create a login and onboarding flow for a fitness app that motivates new users with progress tracking."*

Packaging Designer

1. *"Act as a packaging designer. Design a box concept for a premium tea brand called 'Golden Brew,' focusing on luxury and authenticity."*
2. *"Act as a packaging designer. Suggest a creative pouch design for a line of protein snacks targeting athletes and gym enthusiasts."*
3. *"Act as a packaging designer. Develop a minimalist packaging concept for a tech gadget, ensuring it aligns with modern and clean aesthetics."*

Social Media Graphic Designer

1. *"Act as a social media graphic designer. Create a graphic series for a pet store promoting an upcoming sale, focusing on cute animal imagery and bold calls-to-action."*
2. *"Act as a social media graphic designer. Suggest post ideas for a book club, including a reading challenge graphic and discussion question templates."*
3. *"Act as a social media graphic designer. Design a visually engaging countdown post for the launch of a new product line for a fashion brand."*

Infographic Designer

1. *"Act as an infographic designer. Create a step-by-step infographic for beginners explaining 'How to Start a Podcast.'"*
2. *"Act as an infographic designer. Develop a concept for a comparative infographic showcasing the benefits of electric cars versus traditional vehicles."*
3. *"Act as an infographic designer. Outline an infographic for a health app, visualizing daily habits for better sleep."*

Presentation Designer

1. *"Act as a presentation designer. Create a slide deck theme for a pitch about launching a mobile app for urban gardening."*
2. *"Act as a presentation designer. Develop a visually striking slide*

for showcasing quarterly revenue growth for a tech company."
3. *"Act as a presentation designer. Design a closing slide for a workshop presentation on creativity in business, emphasizing key takeaways."*

Brand Identity Designer

1. *"Act as a brand identity designer. Create a mood board for a luxury wine brand, including logo ideas, color schemes, and typography."*
2. *"Act as a brand identity designer. Propose a full brand kit for an online course platform, focusing on professional and approachable visuals."*
3. *"Act as a brand identity designer. Suggest branding elements for a fitness studio that incorporates mindfulness and yoga."*

Motion Graphics Designer

1. *"Act as a motion graphics designer. Create a concept for a looping animation for a website's hero banner, promoting a travel agency."*
2. *"Act as a motion graphics designer. Suggest a dynamic animation idea for a product explainer video for a tech startup."*
3. *"Act as a motion graphics designer. Outline a storyboard for a 15-second Instagram story animation for a summer clothing collection."*

Typography Specialist

1. *"Act as a typography specialist. Suggest typeface options for an educational children's magazine that balances playfulness and readability."*
2. *"Act as a typography specialist. Recommend creative font treatments for a tech conference's promotional materials, emphasizing innovation."*
3. *"Act as a typography specialist. Provide guidelines for custom lettering for a wedding brand's logo, focusing on elegance and romance."*

Customer Communications

Customer Support Representative

1. *"Act as a customer support representative. Draft a response to a customer who is requesting a refund for a delayed online order, ensuring empathy and professionalism."*
2. *"Act as a customer support representative. Write a follow-up email to a customer who recently submitted a complaint about a defective product, offering a resolution."*
3. *"Act as a customer support representative. Create a script for a live chat agent assisting a customer who is experiencing issues with logging into their account."*

Customer Success Manager

1. "Act as a customer success manager. Draft a personalized onboarding email for a new client who has just signed up for a project management software subscription."
2. "Act as a customer success manager. Create a quarterly check-in email template for a SaaS company to ensure customers are making the most of the product's features."
3. "Act as a customer success manager. Write a proactive email to a customer whose subscription is about to expire, offering renewal options and highlighting new features."

Feedback Collection Specialist

1. "Act as a feedback collection specialist. Create a customer survey email asking for feedback on a recent purchase experience, focusing on product satisfaction and ease of service."
2. "Act as a feedback collection specialist. Draft a friendly email requesting reviews from customers who recently completed a transaction on an e-commerce platform."
3. "Act as a feedback collection specialist. Write a follow-up message thanking a customer for providing feedback and informing them how their suggestions will be implemented."

7

Conclusion: Your AI-Powered Side Hustle Awaits!

This book has taken you on a journey through the exciting world of AI and how you can use it to launch your own side hustle. You've learned that **AI is no longer exclusive to tech experts**; with user-friendly tools and the right guidance, anyone can harness its power.

Let's recap the key takeaways:

- **AI is a powerful tool that can enhance your skills and productivity, not replace them.** You bring the creativity and insights, while AI helps you streamline tasks, generate ideas, and reach new heights.
- **Mastering AI prompt engineering is crucial for unlocking AI's full potential.** By learning how to craft effective prompts, you can get AI to do amazing things, from writing compelling content to designing eye-catching graphics.
- **There are countless AI-powered side hustle opportunities waiting to be explored.** Whether your passion lies in writing, design, automation, or something else entirely,

there's a niche for you in the AI-driven economy.
- **The AI landscape is constantly evolving. Embrace lifelong learning and stay informed about new trends and tools** to maintain a competitive edge in your chosen field.

This isn't just about earning extra income—it's about empowering yourself with skills that will be valuable for years to come. The world of work is changing, and AI is at the forefront of that change. By starting your AI-powered side hustle today, you're not only taking control of your financial future, but also investing in your future-proof skillset.

Don't wait any longer. Take that leap, experiment, and have fun! The opportunities are limitless.

If you found this book helpful in your journey, please consider leaving a review on Amazon. Your feedback helps others discover the power of AI and inspires them to launch their own side hustles.

8

Appendix

- Appendix 1 – 20 Ideas of Interest Areas for AI-powered side hustle
- Appendix 2 - Portfolio of Prompts

9

Resources

- 20 AI Content Generation Tools Every Marketer Needs in 2024. (2024, June 27). Clarity-Ventures.com. https://www.clarity-ventures.com/artificial-intelligence-ecommerce/ai-content-generation-tools
- AI Prompting Best Practices. (n.d.). Codecademy. https://www.codecademy.com/article/ai-prompting-best-practices
- aiparabellum.com. (2024, December 25). What is AI? The Ultimate Guide to Artificial Intelligence. AI Tools Directory | Browse & Find Best AI Tools. https://aiparabellum.com/ai/
- Cyran, R. (2024, May 22). Breakingviews: The $5 trillion AI boom could both succeed and fizzle. Reuters. https://www.reuters.com/breakingviews/5-trln-ai-boom-could-both-succeed-fizzle-2024-05-22
- General Assembly. (2024, September 20). 5 Timeless Prompt Engineering Principles for Reliable AI Outputs.

- General Assembly. https://generalassemb.ly/blog/timeless-prompt-engineering-principles-improve-ai-output-reliability/
- Holdsworth, J. (2024, August 29). Benefits of Chatbots | IBM. Ibm.com. https://www.ibm.com/think/insights/unlocking-the-power-of-chatbots-key-benefits-for-businesses-and-customers
- Jamil Valliani. (2024, September 18). The ultimate guide to writing effective AI prompts - Work Life by Atlassian. Work Life by Atlassian. https://www.atlassian.com/blog/announcements/ultimate-guide-writing-ai-prompts
- Jeff. (2024, March 25). Mastering the perfect prompt formula (for ChatGPT and Google Gemini). Jeff Su. https://www.jeffsu.org/mastering-the-perfect-prompt-formula-for-chatgpt-and-google-gemini/
- Maderis, G. (2023, September 11). 5 benefits of using AI chatbots in customer service. Zendesk. https://www.zendesk.com/blog/5-benefits-using-ai-bots-customer-service/
- Olsen, A. (2024, October 24). Transforming Words into Wonders: Artificial Intelligence for Content Creation - Schmeiser, Olsen & Watts, LLP. Schmeiser, Olsen & Watts, LLP - an Intellectual Property Law Firm. https://iplawusa.com/transforming-words-into-wonders-artificial-intelligence-for-content-creation/
- RPA and AI - The Key to Modern Automation | IT Process Automation. (2024). Softwarehut.com. https://softwarehut.com/blog/tech/rpa-and-ai-the-key-to-automation-in-modern-enterprises
- Shopify. (2024, December 23). 10 Lucrative AI Side Hustles for Entrepreneurs (2024) - Shopify Canada. Shopify. https://www.shopify.com/ca/blog/ai-side-hustles

- Sweenor, D. (2024, December 9). Mind Your AI Manners: The Bottom-Line Impact of Cultural Intelligence. Medium. https://medium.com/@davidsweenor/mind-your-ai-manners-the-bottom-line-impact-of-cultural-intelligence-cbd9468d1810
- Tao, Y., Viberg, O., Baker, R. S., & Kizilcec, R. F. (2024, September 1). Cultural bias and cultural alignment of large language models. PNAS Nexus; Oxford University Press. https://doi.org/10.1093/pnasnexus/pgae346
- The AI Mindset shift: How I use AI every day. (n.d.). Buffer: All-you-need Social Media Toolkit for Small Businesses. https://buffer.com/resources/ai-mindset-shift/
- The Rise of AI-Powered Design Tools: What It Means for Designers. (2024). Kittl.com. https://www.kittl.com/article/ai-in-graphic-design
- The Ultimate Guide to Writing AI Prompts: Examples & Best Practices. (2024). Kipwise.com. https://kipwise.com/blog/ai-prompts
- Verma, A., & Bijja, H. (2024, December 18). AI Myths Debunked: Uncovering the Truth about AI. Pickl.AI. https://www.pickl.ai/blog/ai-myths-debunked/

10

Appendix 1 – 15 Ideas of Interest areas for AI-powered side hustles

Art and Creativity

- Digital arts creator
- Illustrations
- Designer for print-on-demand products

Tutorial – DIY, Crafts, Hobbies

- Online courses
- Youtube videos

Content Creation

- Blogging
- Website design

- Product research for eCommerce

Writing

- Book researcher
- eBook author
- Ghost writer
- Editor

Advertising

- Copywriter
- SEO consulting

Small Business / Home Organization

- Virtual Assistant

11

Appendix 2 – Portfolio of Prompts

APPENDIX 2 – PORTFOLIO OF PROMPTS

Category:

Category:

Category:

Category:

www.ingramcontent.com/pod-product-compliance
Lightning Source LLC
Chambersburg PA
CBHW070411230526
45471CB00006B/2757